Lectionary Worship Aids

*Lent and Easter
Seasons Edition
Cycle C*

for the Revised Common Lectionary

by George Reed, O.S.L.

An Anthology of Worship Resources from
The Immediate Word
a Component of SermonSuite.com
from CSS Publishing Company

CSS Publishing Company, Inc.
Lima, Ohio

LECTIONARY WORSHIP AIDS
LENT AND EASTER SEASONS EDITION, CYCLE C

FIRST EDITION
Copyright © 2013
by CSS Publishing Co., Inc.

Published by CSS Publishing Company, Inc., Lima, Ohio 45807. All rights reserved. No part of this publication may be reproduced in any manner whatsoever without the prior permission of the publisher, except in the case of brief quotations embodied in critical articles and reviews. Inquiries should be addressed to: CSS Publishing Company, Inc., Permissions Department, 5450 N. Dixie Highway, Lima, Ohio 45807.

For more information about CSS Publishing Company resources, visit our website at www.csspub.com or email us at csr@csspub.com or call (800) 241-4056.

ISBN-13: 978-0-7880-2715-4
ISBN-10: 0-7880-2715-8   PRINTED IN USA

*To my wife, Betty,
whose constant love and support has been my greatest joy.*

Table of Contents

Music Resources	6
Introduction	7

Lenten Season

Ash Wednesday	9
Lent 1	14
Lent 2	18
Lent 3	23
Lent 4	28
Lent 5	33
Passion / Palm Sunday	38
Maundy Thursday	43
Good Friday	49

Easter Season

Easter Day	54
Easter 2	58
Easter 3	62
Easter 4	66
Easter 5	71
Easter 6	76
Ascension of Our Lord / Easter 7	80

Music Resources

UMH: United Methodist Hymnal
H82: The Hymnal 1982 (The Episcopal Church)
LBW: Lutheran Book of Worship
PH: Presbyterian Hymnal
CH: Chalice Hymnal
NCH: The New Century Hymnal
NNBH: The New National Baptist Hymnal
AAHH: African-American Heritage Hymnal
CCB: Cokesbury Chorus Book
RENEW: Renew! Songs & Hymns for Blended Worship
ELA: Evangelical Lutheran Worship

Introduction

Early in the history of CSS Publishing Company, we realized that there was a need to provide fresh and relevant worship resources to our customers. Over the years, many different volumes have been developed as an answer to that need. These resources include numerous volumes of *Lectionary Worship Aids*, the *Lectionary Worship Workbook*, and many others.

We live in a world that seems to move faster all the time. Our society continues to react more quickly to the events that go on around us. CSS Publishing has continued to try to fill the need to help pastors relate those current events in their preaching and teaching, so CSS created a unique service called **The Immediate Word**, an integral part of *SermonSuite.com*, to assist pastors in tying important news items to God's word. *SermonSuite.com* is a compilation of preaching and worship material that is presented for timely use each week for the parish pastor. The **TIW** team of practicing parish clergy examines current events each week and seeks God's guidance in connecting the assigned lectionary readings with news and current events happening in the world every day. Even though the worship resources were written for a specific time with **TIW**, the writing is relevant for any and every day.

Included in **The Immediate Word** is a worship resource that helps the parish pastor plan for weekly worship. As with previous volumes in this series, this collection contains resources such as calls to worship, hymn selections, and prayers that relate to the lectionary for each week.

This volume contains a collection of these resources for Cycle C of the Revised Common Lectionary that has been gleaned from **The Immediate Word**. It is our prayer that this resource will prove to be an invaluable asset to the success of your ministry.

The editors of CSS Publishing Company, Inc.

Ash Wednesday

Joel 2:1-2, 12-17
2 Corinthians 5:20b—6:10
Matthew 6:1-6, 16-21

Call to Worship
Leader: Have mercy on us, O God, according to your steadfast love;
People: according to your abundant mercy, blot out our transgressions.
Leader: Purge us with hyssop, and we shall be clean;
People: wash us, and we shall be whiter than snow.
Leader: Restore to us the joy of your salvation
People: and sustain in us a willing spirit.

OR

Leader: Return to your God, for God is gracious and merciful, slow to anger,
People: and abounding in steadfast love and relents from punishing.
Leader: Gather the people, sanctify the congregation,
People: assemble the aged, gather the children.
Leader: Spare your people, O God!
People: Let us return to God with all our hearts!

Hymns and Sacred Songs
"Lord, Who Throughout These Forty Days"
found in:
UMH: 269   NCH: 211
H82: 142   CH: 180
PH: 81

"Only Trust Him"
found in:
UMH: 337   NNBH: 193
AAHH: 369

"Where He Leads Me"
found in:
UMH: 338   NNBH: 229
AAHH: 550   CH: 346

"Spirit Song"
found in:
UMH: 347   CH: 352
AAHH: 321

"Softly and Tenderly"
found in:
UMH: 348   NCH: 449
AAHH: 347   CH: 340
NNBH: 168   ELW: 608

"Just As I Am, Without One Plea"
found in:
UMH: 357   NCH: 207
H82: 693   CH: 339
PH: 370   LBW: 296
AAHH: 344/345   ELW: 592
NNBH: 167

"Love Divine, All Loves Excelling"
found in:
UMH: 384   NCH: 43
H82: 657   CH: 517
PH: 376   LBW: 315

AAHH: 440   ELW: 631
NNBH: 65

"Jesus Calls Us"
found in:
UMH: 398   CH: 337
H82: 549/550   LBW: 494
NNBH: 183   ELW: 696
NCH: 171/172

"As the Deer"
found in:
CCB: 83   Renew: 9

"Refiner's Fire"
found in:
CCB: 79

Prayer for the Day / Collect
O God, who desires life for your children, grant us the grace to return to you that we may find life abundant and joyful; through Jesus Christ our Savior. Amen.

OR

We come to you, O God, to acknowledge that we are but dust of the earth unless you breathe your life and Spirit into us. May this season of Lent be to us a new beginning as we turn to you and to life eternal. Amen.

Prayer of Confession
Leader: Let us confess to God and before one another our sins and especially our constant wandering from the paths of life to the ways of death.

People: We confess to you, O God, and before one another that we have sinned. You have set before us the way to life eternal and yet we choose paths that lead us to destruction. You made us in your image of love and yet we are able to see others in hunger, pain, and poverty but we do nothing to help. We have failed to be your people. We have failed to act as the body of Christ. Forgive us and return us to your paths that we may join our Savior in reaching out to others in love. Amen.
Leader: God is always calling us back to love and to life. God's is faithful to forgive and redeem. Rejoice in God's love.

Prayers of the People (and the Lord's Prayer)
Praised and wondrous is your name, O God, who has created us and who has redeemed us. We praise your for your loving kindness to all you have created.

(The following paragraph may be used if a separate prayer of confessions has not been used.)
We confess to you, O God, and before one another that we have sinned. You have set before us the way to life eternal and yet we choose paths that lead us to destruction. You made us in your image of love and yet we are able to see others in hunger, pain, and poverty but we do nothing to help. We have failed to be your people. We have failed to act as the body of Christ. Forgive us and return us to your paths that we may join our Savior in reaching out to others in love.

We give you thanks for this time of Lent, which calls us back, once again, to you and to life. We thank you for the faithfulness of the church throughout the ages to call your people to repentance and new life.

(Other thanksgivings may be offered.)

We pray for ourselves, your church around the world, and all your creation. Help us, who own the name of Christ, to make this a time of true repentance that we may faithfully be the body of Christ to those around us.

(Other intercessions may be offered.)
All these things we ask in the name of our Savior Jesus Christ, who taught us to pray together, saying:
Our Father... Amen.

(Or if the Lord's Prayer is not used at this point in the service.)
All this we ask in the name of the Blessed and Holy Trinity. Amen.

Lent 1

Deuteronomy 26:1-11
Romans 10:8b-13
Luke 4:1-13

Call to Worship
Leader: God comes among us in our worship.
People: We will draw near and listen to our God.
Leader: God comes among us in our joys.
People: We will draw near and see what God is doing.
Leader: God draws near us in our wilderness experiences.
People: We will draw near and in silence wait on God.

Hymns and Sacred Songs
"Lord, Who Throughout These Forty Days"
found in:
UMH: 269   NCH: 211
H82: 142   CH: 180
PH: 81

"Come Out the Wilderness"
found in:
UMH: 416   AAHH: 367

"Be Still, My Soul"
found in:
UMH: 534   NCH: 488
AAHH: 135   LBW: 566
NNBH: 263

"Stand By Me"
found in:

UMH: 512   CH: 629
NNBH: 318

"Out of the Depths I Cry to You"
found in:
UMH: 515   NCH: 483
H82: 666   CH: 510
PH: 240   LBW: 295

"O Thou, in Whose Presence"
found in:
UMH: 518

"Saranam, Saranam"
found in:
UMH: 523

"Nearer, My God, to Thee"
found in:
UMH: 528   NCH: 606
AAHH: 163   CH: 577
NNBH: 314

"Through It All"
found in:
UMH: 507   CH: 555
NNBH: 402   CCB: 61

"All I Need Is You"
found in:
CCB: 100

"You Are Mine"
found in:
CCB: 58

Prayer for the Day / Collect
O God, who created us for your loving companionship, grant us the grace to be silent in the wilderness time of our lives that we may more clearly perceive your presence among and within us; through Jesus Christ our Savior. Amen.

OR

We have come into your presence, O God, to worship you and to praise your holy name. We have come to offer ourselves to your service as we follow our Savior Jesus. Help us to be willing to enter the wilderness of our lives with him and quietly await what you would reveal to us. Amen.

Prayer of Confession
Leader: Let us confess to God and before one another our sins and especially our tendency to take the easy way out.
People: We confess to you, O God, and before one another that we have sinned. When life gets rough and we become uncomfortable, we forget to seek you and your ways which will lead to life and spiritual growth. Instead, we seek the easy way out. We want to cover over the emptiness and silence, instead of finding you and allowing you to fill the void. Forgive us and grant us the faith to wait in silence for you to speak to us once more your message of life and hope. Amen.
Leader: God is always waiting for us and is always ready to be with us in all of our lives. Know that God loves us, forgives us, and gives us his Spirit to guide us into new life.

Prayers of the People (and the Lord's Prayer)
We praise and adore you, O God, for your steadfast love that never leaves us nor fails us. You are the constant one who never changes and who is closer to us than our own breath.

(The following paragraph may be used if a separate prayer of confession has not been used.)
We confess to you, O God, and before one another that we have sinned. When life gets rough and we become uncomfortable, we forget to seek you and your ways that will lead to life and spiritual growth. Instead, we seek the easy way out. We want to cover over the emptiness and silence, instead of finding you and allowing you to fill the void. Forgive us and grant us the faith to wait in silence for you to speak to us once more your message of life and hope.

We thank you for the ways you communicate your presence to us. We thank you for the way the scripture comes alive with your Spirit and for the times of communion in prayer. We thank you for the sacraments, which become so powerful with your presence. We thank you for all the times you have been with us when we have not even been aware that you were working within us.

(Other thanksgivings may be offered.)
We pray for all, anywhere, who are in the wilderness experience. We pray that as you are with them in that time, they will be aware of you. We ask that you would make us sensitive to those around us so that when they are crossing the desert, we can be there to offer a bit of shade and cup of cool water.

(Other intercessions may be offered.)
All these things we ask in the name of our Savior Jesus Christ, who taught us to pray together, saying:
Our Father... Amen.

(Or if the Lord's Prayer is not used at this point in the service)
All this we ask in the name of the Blessed and Holy Trinity. Amen.

Lent 2

Genesis 15:1-12, 17-18
Philippians 3:17—4:1
Luke 13:31-35

Call to Worship
Leader: God is our light and our salvation;
People: whom shall we fear?
Leader: God is the stronghold of our lives;
People: of whom shall we be afraid?
Leader: One thing we ask of our God;
People: that we may dwell in God's presence always.

OR

Leader: God invites us to come and worship.
People: We come to worship our Creator.
Leader: God invites us to join in creating.
People: We unite with God in building God's reign.
Leader: God calls us to create together.
People: With one another we will serve God and humanity.

Hymns and Sacred Songs
"All Creatures of Our God and King"
found in:
UMH: 62   NCH: 17
H82: 400   CH: 22
PH: 455   LBW: 527
AAHH: 147   Renew: 47
NNBH: 33

"Maker, in Whom We Live"
found in:
UMH: 88

"For the Beauty of the Earth"
found in:
UMH: 92   NCH: 28
H82: 416   CH: 56
PH: 473   LBW: 561
NNBH: 8

"For the Fruits of this Creation"
found in:
UMH: 97   NCH: 425
H82: 424   CH: 714
PH: 553   LBW: 563

"God of the Sparrow, God of the Whale"
found in:
UMH: 122   NCH: 32
PH: 272   CH: 70

"O God of Every Nation"
found in:
UMH: 435   CH: 310
H82: 607   LBW: 416
PH: 289

"Behold a Broken World"
found in:
UMH: 426

"Let There Be Light"
found in:

UMH: 440   CH: 589
NCH: 450

"For the Gift of Creation"
found in:
CCB: 67

"Refiner's Fire"
found in:
CCB: 79

Prayer for the Day / Collect
O God, who created us to be co-creators with you, grant us the wisdom and courage to be part of making the world better rather than just complaining about the state of the world; through Jesus Christ our Savior. Amen.

OR

As you come among us this day, our Creator and redeemer, we offer you our praise and adoration for your creating powers. We ask you to re-create us more fully into your image that we may meaningfully participate in your bringing your creation to the fullness of your dream. Amen.

Prayer of Confession
Leader: Let us confess to God and before one another our sins and especially the ways we are so quick to be critical and so slow to do the work of solving the problem.
People: We confess to you, O God, and before one another that we have sinned. You have created us to join in bringing your creation to its fullness, but we spend most of our time complaining about the way things are without offering any ideas or any help. We want to judge the ways things are, but we don't want to take responsibility

for making it better. Forgive us and send the power of your creating Spirit to fill us and empower us to live into the image you created for us. Amen.
Leader: God desires nothing more than bringing creation to its fullness. When we are willing to be a part of that process, both by being transformed and transforming the world, God joyfully accepts our participation.

Prayers of the People (and the Lord's Prayer)
We praise you, O God, for the wonders of your creating power. We are in awe of the magnitude of creation. We are in awe that you have made us to be your co-creators.

(The following paragraph may be used if a separate prayer of confession has not been used.)
We confess to you, O God, and before one another that we have sinned. You have created us to join in bringing your creation to its fullness, but we spend most of our time complaining about the way things are without offering any ideas or any help. We want to judge the ways things are, but we don't want to take responsibility for making it better. Forgive us and send the power of your creating Spirit to fill us and empower us to live in the image you created for us.

We give you thanks for the power of creation that you have shared with your children. We thank you for our ability to think and analyze and bring forth new thoughts and new solutions. We thank you for the ways we find you in the midst of this process.

(Other thanksgivings may be offered.)
We pray for those who are stuck and find it so difficult to make something worthwhile out of their lives. We pray that as your Spirit works within them to inspire them, you will help us to create the systems and situations where their work can be fruitful.

(Other intercessions may be offered.)
All these things we ask in the name of our Savior Jesus Christ, who taught us to pray together, saying:
Our Father... Amen.

(Or if the Lord's Prayer is not used at this point in the service)
All this we ask in the name of the Blessed and Holy Trinity. Amen.

Lent 3

Isaiah 55:1-9
1 Corinthians 10:1-13
Luke 13:1-9

Call to Worship
Leader: Behold the power and glory of our God!
People: God's steadfast love is better than life itself.
Leader: Let us bless God as long as we live.
People: We lift up our hands and call on God's name.
Leader: In the shadow of God's wings, let us sing for joy.
People: We cling to God, whose right hand upholds us.

OR

Leader: Come into the presence of our God.
People: But we are sinful and unfaithful people.
Leader: God knows that and God loves us anyway.
People: We are truly sorry for our unfaithfulness and sin.
Leader: God invites us to not only be sorry but also to be made new.
People: We will turn to God and live as God's children.

Hymns and Sacred Songs
"Dear Lord and Father of Mankind"
found in:
UMH: 358   NCH: 502
H82: 652/653   CH: 594
PH: 345   LBW: 506

"It's Me, It's Me, O Lord"
found in:

UMH: 352   CH: 579
NNBH: 496

"I Surrender All"
found in:
UMH: 354   NNBH: 198
AAHH: 396

"Spirit of the Living God"
found in:
UMH: 393   NCH: 283
PH: 322   CH: 259
AAHH: 320   Renew: 90
NNBH: 133

"Take My Life and Let It Be"
found in:
UMH: 399   NCH: 448
H82: 707   CH: 609
PH: 391   LBW: 406
NNBH: 213   Renew: 150

"Lord, I Want to Be a Christian"
found in:
UMH: 402   NCH: 454
PH: 372   CH: 589
AAHH: 463   Renew: 145
NNBH: 156

"I Want to Walk As a Child of the Light"
found in:
UMH: 206   Renew: 152
H82: 490

"O Master, Let Me Walk with Thee"
found in:
UMH: 430 NCH: 503
H82: 659/660 CH: 602
PH: 357 LBW: 492
NNBH: 445

"Refiner's Fire"
found in:
CCB: 79

"Change My Heart, O God"
found in:
CCB: 56 Renew: 143

Prayer for the Day / Collect
O God, who calls your children to turn and walk in the way of life, grant us the courage to truly repent, to turn our lives to face you and walk in new paths; through Jesus Christ our Savior. Amen.

OR

We come into your presence, O God, that we may amend our lives and live as Jesus taught and showed us. Amen.

Prayer of Confession
Leader: Let us confess to God and before one another our sins and especially the ease with which we say we are sorry for the things we said and did though we seldom change our way of living.
People: We confess to you, O God, and before one another that we have sinned. We have been unfaithful to you and hurtful to one another. We have said we are sorry when we have had no intention of changing. We have

said we are sorry when we intended to change, but have not changed. We are more interested in people thinking we are good than we are in actually being good. Forgive us and make us bold to turn our lives around and live fully in your presence. Amen.

Leader: God desires that we live in wholeness and peace. God welcomes our confession and empowers us with the Spirit to become the children of God we truly are.

Prayers of the People (and the Lord's Prayer)
We raise our voices in praise to you, our God and teacher, for you are the one who lives in wholeness and holiness. Your actions are one with your intentions. You desire that we would live the same way.

(The following paragraph may be used if a separate prayer of confession has not been used.)
We confess to you, O God, and before one another that we have sinned. We have been unfaithful to you and hurtful to one another. We have said we are sorry when we had no intention of changing. We have said we are sorry when we intended to change, but have not changed. We are more interested in people thinking we are good than we are in actually being good. Forgive us and make us bold to turn our lives around and live fully in your presence.

We give you thanks for all the ways you lead us into a full and abundant life. We thank you for the scriptures and the traditions of the church, which help us to understand your desires for us. We thank you for the teachings and life of Jesus and for the Spirit that guides and empowers us.

(Other thanksgivings may be offered.)
We pray for those who find themselves lost in this world without direction. We pray that we may be faithful in following you, so that our lives may serve as a pattern for them.

(Other intercessions may be offered.)
All these things we ask in the name of our Savior Jesus Christ, who taught us to pray together, saying:
Our Father... Amen.

(Or if the Lord's Prayer is not used at this point in the service)
All this we ask in the name of the Blessed and Holy Trinity. Amen.

Lent 4

Joshua 5:9-12
2 Corinthians 5:16-21
Luke 15:1-3, 11b-32

Call to Worship
Leader: Happy are we whose transgression is forgiven,
People: happy are we whose sin is covered.
Leader: Let all who are faithful offer prayer to God.
People: Let us listen to the counsel of our God.
Leader: Be glad in God and rejoice, O righteous,
People: and shout for joy, all you upright in heart.

OR

Leader: Come, let us celebrate our prodigal God.
People: God is prodigal? How is that?
Leader: To be prodigal is to be extravagant, free-handed.
People: Then our God is certainly prodigal!
Leader: We are blessed to have a God who gives so freely.
People: Let us thank God and show we are God's children by our liberality.

Hymns and Sacred Songs
"What Wondrous Love Is This"
found in:
UMH: 292   CH: 200
H82: 439   LBW: 385
PH: 85   ELW: 666
NCH: 223

"Lift High the Cross"
found in:

UMH: 159
H82: 473
PH: 371
AAHH: 242

NCH: 198
CH: 108
LBW: 377
ELW: 660

"How Can We Name a Love"
found in:
UMH: 111

"Love Divine, All Loves Excelling"
found in:
UMH: 384
H82: 657
PH: 376
AAHH: 440
NNBH: 65

NCH: 43
CH: 517
LBW: 315
ELW: 631

"O Love Divine, What Hast Thou Done"
found in:
UMH: 287

"The Care the Eagle Gives Her Young"
found in:
UMH: 118
NCH: 468

CH: 76

"O Love, How Deep"
found in:
UMH: 267
H82: 448/449
PH: 83

NCH: 209
LBW: 88
ELW: 322

"In the Cross of Christ I Glory"
found in:
UMH: 295

NCH: 193/194

H82: 441/442 LBW: 104
PH: 84 ELW: 324
NNBH: 104

"I Am Loved"
found in:
CCB: 80

"O How He Love You and Me!"
found in:
CCB: 38 Renew: 27

Prayer for the Day / Collect
O God, who is our prodigal parent, grant us the grace to be as recklessly extravagant with love, grace, and kindness to others as you have been to us; through Jesus Christ our Savior. Amen.

OR

We come into your presence, O God of prodigal love, to offer praise and thanksgiving for your graciousness. We pray that we, too, may be prodigal in giving to others the love, grace, and kindness you have given to us. Amen.

Prayer of Confession
Leader: Let us confess to God and before one another our sins and especially our quickness to receive forgiveness and our slowness to offer it.
People: We confess to you, O God, and before one another that we have sinned. You have been so extravagant with your grace and forgiveness toward us and we have been so slow to forgive others. We remember hurts old and new as if they all happened just yesterday. We assume that those who have hurt us have done so intentionally,

while excusing the things we do against others. Forgive us and so fill us with your Spirit that our forgiveness may be as extravagant and ready as yours. Amen.
Leader: God's forgiveness is extravagant for all, even though we don't deserve it. Receive God's forgiveness and pass it on to others.

Prayers of the People (and the Lord's Prayer)
We worship and adore you, O God, for your abundant, extravagant love that you lavish on all your creation.

(The following paragraph may be used if a separate prayer of confession has not been used.)
We confess to you, O God, and before one another that we have sinned. You have been so extravagant with your grace and forgiveness toward us and we have been so slow to forgive others. We remember hurts old and new as if they all happened just yesterday. We assume that those who have hurt us have done so intentionally, while excusing the things we do against others. Forgive us and so fill us with your Spirit that our forgiveness may be as extravagant and ready as yours.
    We thank you for all the ways you have shown us your love. We thank you for creation and for the gift of life. We thank you for your church and its witness to your love. Most of all we thank you for Jesus who brought your love to us in human flesh.

(Other thanksgivings may be offered.)
We pray for one another in our need and for all your children. We know that many find it hard to understand that there is a loving God when life seems so hateful. We pray that we, as your church, may be so faithful to you and your mission that all will soon know the joy of your reign on earth.

(Other intercessions may be offered.)
All these things we ask in the name of our Savior Jesus Christ, who taught us to pray together, saying:
Our Father... Amen.

(Or if the Lord's Prayer is not used at this point in the service)
All this we ask in the name of the Blessed and Holy Trinity. Amen.

Lent 5

Isaiah 43:16-21
Philippians 3:4b-14
John 12:1-8

Call to Worship
Leader: When God restored us, we were like those who dream.
People: Then our mouths were filled with laughter, and our tongues with shouts of joy.
Leader: God has done great things for us and we rejoiced.
People: Restore our fortunes, O God, like the watercourses in the Negeb.
Leader: May those who sow in tears reap with shouts of joy.
People: Those who go out weeping, bearing the seed for sowing, shall come home with shouts of joy, carrying their sheaves.

OR

Leader: Come to God and find your true home.
People: We have tried to come home and we have gotten lost.
Leader: The world has changed. God has opened new paths.
People: We like the old way with which we are comfortable.
Leader: But the old, comfortable ways don't work for those you need to lead to God.
People: We will take the new ways so that we can lead all God's children home.

Hymns and Sacred Songs
"Marching to Zion"
found in:
UMH: 733

"Come, We that Love the Lord"
found in:
UMH: 732   NNBH: 36
H82: 392   NCH: 379/380
AAHH: 590   CH: 707

"Come Sunday"
found in:
UMH: 728

"Arise, Shine Out, Your Light Has Come"
found in:
UMH: 725   Renew: 123
PH: 411

"Happy the Home When God Is There"
found in:
UMH: 445

"We Utter Our Cry"
found in:
UMH: 439

"Let There Be Peace on Earth"
found in:
UMH: 431   CH: 677

"Pues Si Vivimos" ("When We Are Living")
found in:

UMH: 356　　　　　　　　CH: 536
PH: 400

"Sanctuary"
found in:
CCB: 87　　　　　　　　Renew: 185

"Your Loving Kindness Is Better than Life"
found in:
CCB: 26

Prayer for the Day / Collect
O God, in whom we live and move and have our being, grant us the wisdom and courage to come home to you; through Jesus Christ our Savior. Amen.

OR

We come to worship the one in whom we live and move and have our being. We ask for the power and guidance of the Spirit to help us understand where we are and how we need to go in order to reach home. We pray for the courage to receive new directions. Amen.

Prayer of Confession
Leader: Let us confess to God and before one another our sins and especially the way we cling to old ways that do not work when God is offering us new life.
People: We confess to you, O God, and before one another that we have sinned. Though we are your children and talk about coming to your house for worship, our lives betray our lostness and we seek places other than your presence to fill our lives with meaning. We look to wealth, power, and status, but we also use good things to mask our need for you as we try to substitute family and

friends and good deeds. Help us to understand that it is only in you that we can be the best family member, the best friend, and do the truly good deeds. Amen.
Leader: God is always seeking for his children to return home. Receive the power of God's Spirit as you return to God and begin to shine with the light of God within you.

Prayers of the People (and the Lord's Prayer)
We worship and adore you, the ground of our being and the depth of our lives. From your breath, your Spirit, and your life, we were created. We belong to you and in you.

(The following paragraph may be used if a separate prayer of confession has not been used.)
We confess to you, O God, and before one another that we have sinned. Though we are your children and talk about coming to your house for worship, our lives betray our lostness and we seek places other than your presence to fill our lives with meaning. We look to wealth, power, and status, but we also use good things to mask our need for you as we try to substitute family and friends and good deeds. Help us to understand that it is only in you that we can be the best family member, the best friend, and do the truly good deeds.

We give you thanks for all the ways you have called us to yourself. You have sent us prophets and seers, psalmist and apostles. Most of all, you have sent us Jesus to show us what it means to live in you.

(Other thanksgivings may be offered.)
We pray for those in need and especially for those who are striving to find their home. As you call them to yourself, so fill us with your Spirit that we may be beacons that help them find their way to you.

(Other intercessions may be offered.)
All these things we ask in the name of our Savior Jesus Christ, who taught us to pray together, saying:
Our Father... Amen.

(Or if the Lord's Prayer is not used at this point in the service)
All this we ask in the name of the Blessed and Holy Trinity. Amen.

Passion / Palm Sunday

Isaiah 50:4-9a
Philippians 2:5-11
Luke 22:14—23:56

Call to Worship
Leader: Give thanks to God, for God is good;
People: God's love endures forever.
Leader: Open the gates of righteousness,
People: that we may enter and give thanks.
Leader: This is the day that God has made;
People: we will rejoice and be glad in it.

OR

Leader: Be gracious to us, O God, for we are in distress;
People: our souls and bodies waste away from grief.
Leader: Our lives are spent with sorrows,
People: and our years spent with sighing.
Leader: But we trust in you, O God.
People: We say, "You are our God."

Hymns and Sacred Songs
"Weary of All Trumpeting"
found in:
UMH: 442   H82: 572

"O Young and Fearless Prophet"
found in:
UMH: 444   CH: 669

"Dear Jesus, in Whose Life I See"
found in:
UMH: 468

"Close to Thee"
found in:
UMH: 407   NNBH: 317
AAHH: 552/553

"Seek Ye First"
found in:
UMH: 405   PH: 333
H82: 711   CH: 354

"Take Up Thy Cross"
found in:
UMH: 415   PH: 393
H82: 675   LBW: 398

"Make Me a Captive, Lord"
found in:
UMH: 421   PH: 378

"Take My Life, and Let It Be"
found in:
UMH: 399   NCH: 448
H82: 707   CH: 609
PH: 391   LBW: 406
NNBH: 213   Renew: 150

"Walk with Me"
found in:
CCB: 88

"We Are His Hands"
found in:
CCB: 85

Prayer for the Day / Collect
O God, who makes a path of righteousness and peace in the midst of evil and war, grant us the courage to follow our Savior Jesus as he brings your reign into the midst of the powers that oppose you; through Jesus Christ our Savior. Amen.

OR

We come to join with Jesus as he enters into Jerusalem and makes his stand against evil power and injustice. Help us to not be those who wave their palms but refuse to enter into the sufferings of our Savior. Fill us with courage that we may be true disciples of Jesus. Amen.

Prayer of Confession
Leader: Let us confess to God and before one another our sins and especially the way we speak of our faith so assuredly yet walk the path of Jesus with so much hesitation.
People: We confess to you, O God, and before one another that we have sinned. We are quick to claim our place with Jesus when it enhances our standing with others, but we are loathe to follow him when it costs us friends and popularity. We take the name of Jesus when it makes us look holy and upstanding, but when his values go against the mainstream of society, we hesitate to take a stand. Forgive us and empower us with your Spirit, O God, that we may claim Jesus with our actions as well as with our words. Amen.
Leader: God loves us and is always ready to assist us when we wish to follow the ways of justice, mercy, and humility.

May the Spirit of our God fill you with courage and resolve to follow Jesus.

Prayers of the People (and the Lord's Prayer)
All glory, honor, and power are yours, O God, by right, because you are the Creator and redeemer of all creation. When the powers of evil rise up, you send your Son and your people to stand against them. You are the one who demands justice and mercy for all creation.

(The following paragraph may be used if a separate prayer of confession has not been used.)
We confess to you, O God, and before one another that we have sinned. We are quick to claim our place with Jesus when it enhances our standing with others, but we are loath to follow him when it costs us friends and popularity. We take the name of Jesus when it makes us look holy and upstanding, but when his values go against the mainstream of society, we hesitate to take a stand. Forgive us and empower us with your Spirit, O God, that we may claim Jesus with our actions as well as with our words.

We give you thanks for all the ways you bring your steadfast love and kindness to us and to all creation. We thank you for the opportunities you give us to stand with Jesus on the side of those who are oppressed and misused.

(Other thanksgivings may be offered.)
We pray for your reign to come in its fullness and for us to be faithful servants of you by being faithful caretakers of one another and of all creation.

(Other intercessions may be offered.)
All these things we ask in the name of our Savior Jesus Christ, who taught us to pray together, saying:
Our Father... Amen.

(Or if the Lord's Prayer is not used at this point in the service)
All this we ask in the name of the Blessed and Holy Trinity. Amen.

Maundy Thursday

Exodus 12:1-4 (5-10) 11-14
1 Corinthians 11:23-26
John 13:1-17, 31b-25

Call to Worship
Leader: What shall we return to God for all this bounty to me?
People: We will lift up the cup of salvation and call on the name of our God.
Leader: Let us pay our vows to God in the presence of all the people.
People: We will offer to God a thanksgiving sacrifice.
Leader: Let us call on the name of our God.
People: We will pay our vows to God in the presence of all the people.

OR

Footwashing
Leader: Come into the presence of our Savior.
People: We come to worship and praise the Christ.
Leader: See him kneel before you and wash your feet.
People: We are humbled beyond thought at this.
Leader: See him hand you the basin and towel.
People: We go where he sends us to serve others.

OR

Eucharist
Leader: Come into the presence of our Savior.
People: We come to worship and praise the Christ.
Leader: See him give you his body and blood.

People: We are truly humbled by his sacrifice.
Leader: Now he sends you to give yourself to others.
People: We go where he sends us to give ourselves in the name of the Christ.

Hymns and Sacred Songs
"Go to Dark Gethsemane"
found in:
UMH: 290   CH: 196
H82: 171   LBW: 109
PH: 97   ELW: 347
NCH: 219

"Jesu, Jesu"
found in:
UMH: 432   CH: 600
H82: 602   ELW: 708
PH: 367   CCB: 66
NCH: 498   Renew: 289

"For the Bread Which You Have Broken"
found in:
UMH: 614/615   CH: 411
H82: 340/341   LBW: 200
PH: 508/509   ELW: 494

"Lord, Whose Love Through Humble Service"
found in:
UMH: 582   LBW: 423
H82: 610   ELW: 712
PH: 427   Renew: 286
CH: 461

"Let Us Break Bread Together on Our Knees"
found in:

UMH: 618
H82: 325
PH: 513
AAHH: 686
NNBH: 358

NCH: 330
CH: 425
LBW: 212
ELW: 471
CCB: 46

"Now the Silence"
found in:
UMH: 619
H82: 333
CH: 415

LBW: 205
ELW: 460
Renew: 221

"Here, O My Lord, I See Thee"
found in:
UMH: 623
H82: 318
PH: 520

NCH: 336
CH: 416
LBW: 211

"Lord, Speak to Me"
found in:
UMH: 463
PH: 426

NCH: 531
ELW: 676

"Make Me a Servant"
found in:
CCB: 90

"We Are His Hands"
found in:
CCB: 85

Prayer for the Day / Collect
Footwashing
O God, who has come among us as a servant, grant us the

grace to kneel before you in worship and to kneel before others in service; through Jesus Christ our Savior. Amen.

OR

We come, O God, to remember and celebrate that night when Jesus knelt at the feet of his disciples and washed their feet. Help us as we bow before your holiness that we may learn to kneel in service as our Savior Jesus did. Amen.

Eucharist
O God, who has come to give yourself to us, grant us the grace to receive you into our hearts so that we may give ourselves to others: through Jesus Christ our Savior. Amen.

OR

We come, O God, to remember and celebrate the night when Jesus offered himself to his disciples at the Last Supper. Help us as we receive him into ourselves that we may give ourselves in service to others. Amen.

Prayer of Confession
Leader: Let us confess to God and before one another our sins, especially our pride.
People: We confess to you, O God, and before one another that we have sinned. We come to worship our Savior, Jesus, who knelt and washed his disciples' feet and then offered himself to them in that first communion service, and yet we are too proud to follow his example. We are more apt to look down on others than to kneel at their feet. We are more likely to use others than to serve them. We are more prone to take from others than to give to them. Forgive us our arrogant ways and draw us back to

Jesus' side where we may learn to humbly worship you and humbly serve others. Amen.
Leader: Jesus, the humble one, is always ready to receive us. He welcomes us to himself and sends us out to serve others.

Prayers of the People (and the Lord's Prayer)
We come to worship and adore you, O God, for your steadfast love and grace toward us and all your creation. We praise you for your love that gives itself to us over and over again.

(The following paragraph may be used if a separate prayer of confessions has not been used.)
We confess to you, O God, and before one another that we have sinned. We come to worship our Savior, Jesus, who knelt and washed his disciples' feet and then offered himself to them in that first communion service, and yet we are too proud to follow his example. We are more apt to look down on others than to kneel at their feet. We are more likely to use others than to serve them. We are more prone to take from others than to give to them. Forgive us our arrogant ways and draw us back to Jesus' side where we may learn to humbly worship you and humbly serve others.

We give you thanks for all the ways in which you come to us and bring us your gracious love. We thank you for the example of service Jesus has set for us and for his example of sacrificial giving.

(Other thanksgivings may be offered.)
We pray with Jesus for the church and for the world. We pray that we may be faithful as your people, your children, and your image. We pray that our faithful service to the world will draw it closer to you, life, and wholeness.

(Other intercessions may be offered.)
All these things we ask in the name of our Savior Jesus

Christ, who taught us to pray together, saying:
Our Father... Amen.

(Or if the Lord's Prayer is not used at this point in the service.)
All this we ask in the name of the Blessed and Holy Trinity. Amen.

Good Friday

Isaiah 52:13—53:12
Hebrews 10:16-25
John 18:1—19:42

Call to Worship
Leader: O my God, I cry by day, but you do not answer;
People: and by night, but I find no rest.
Leader: Yet you are holy, enthroned on the praises of Israel.
People: In you our ancestors trusted.
Leader: Do not be far from me,
People: for trouble is near and there is no one to help.

OR

Leader: Come and stand beneath the cross of Jesus.
People: We come reluctantly because we prefer Easter to Good Friday.
Leader: Come and stand under the love and care of our God.
People: We come in awe that we could be loved like this!
Leader: Come and know that you are God's beloved children.
People: May we share that knowledge with all God's people.

Hymns and Sacred Songs
"O Sacred Head, Now Wounded"
found in:
UMH: 286	NCH: 226
H82: 168/169	CH: 202
PH: 98	LBW: 116/117

AAHH: 250 ELW: 351/352
NNBH: 108 Renew: 235

"What Wondrous Love Is This"
found in:
UMH: 292 CH: 200
H82: 439 LBW: 385
PH: 85 ELW: 666
NCH: 223 Renew: 277

"In the Cross of Christ I Glory"
found in:
UMH: 295 NCH: 193/194
H82: 441/442 LBW: 104
PH: 84 ELW: 324
NNBH: 104

"Ah, Holy Jesus"
found in:
UMH: 289 CH: 210
H82: 158 LBW: 123
PH: 93 ELW: 349
NCH: 218 Renew: 183

"Beneath the Cross of Jesus"
found in:
UMH: 297 NCH: 190
H82: 498 CH: 197
PH: 92 LBW: 107
AAHH: 247 ELW: 338
NNBH: 106

"Were You There"
found in:
UMH: 288 NCH: 229

H82: 172   CH: 198
PH: 102   LBW: 92
AAHH: 254   ELW: 363
NNBH: 109

"Alas! And Did My Saviour Bleed"
found in:
UMH: 294/359   CH: 204
PH: 78   LBW: 98
AAHH: 263/264   ELW: 337
NCH: 199/200

"When I Survey the Wondrous Cross"
found in:
UMH: 298/299   NCH: 224
H82: 474   CH: 195
PH: 100/101   LBW: 482
AAHH: 243   ELW: 803
NNBH: 113   Renew: 236

"O How He Loves You and Me!"
found in:
CCB: 38   Renew: 27

"Only by Grace"
found in:
CCB: 42

Prayer for the Day / Collect
O God, who is love unbounded and eternal, grant us the grace to remember this day with gratitude for your loving kindness to us and to all your creation; through Jesus Christ our Savior. Amen.

OR

We have come this day, O God, to reflect upon the costly sacrifice that love is ever-ready to make for the beloved. Give us grateful hearts to worship you, the giver of love and life. Amen.

Prayer of Confession
Leader: Let us confess to God and before one another our sins and especially our unwillingness to risk ourselves in love.
People: We confess to you, O God, and before one another that we have sinned. We want to be safe. We avoid pain and even being uncomfortable at all costs. We have lost any sense of the common good and are interested only in our own good and that of those closest to us. The whole idea of sacrifice is beyond our comprehension. We are willing to give up little, if anything, for others especially if the others are strangers. Forgive us and call us back to the cross of Jesus so we may see that sacrifice is sometimes the only answer. Make us bold to go forth for you no matter what the cost. Amen.
Leader: God gives all for us. God's love and forgiveness are never ending. Share that with others, even strangers.

Prayers of the People (and the Lord's Prayer)
We praise your name, O God, and glorify you for your ever-giving love for us and for all your creation. You have shown us that there is no limit to your love for us.

(The following paragraph may be used if a separate prayer of confession has not been used.)
We confess to you, O God, and before one another that we have sinned. We want to be safe. We avoid pain and even being uncomfortable at all costs. We have lost any sense of the common good and are interested only in our own good and that of those closest to us. The whole idea of sacrifice is

beyond our comprehension. We are willing to give up little, if anything, for others especially if the others are strangers. Forgive us and call us back to the cross of Jesus so we may see that sacrifice is sometimes the only answer. Make us bold to go forth for you no matter what the cost.

    We give you thanks for your love and care. We thank you for your church and those within it who have been willing to sacrifice in order for us to come to know you. We thank you for those who have loved us when we have been unlovable and have thus shown us your love.

(Other thanksgivings may be offered.)
We pray for those who are in need. We pray especially for those whose needs have not been met because we have refused to sacrifice our wants to help them in their needs. We pray for ourselves that we might better reflect the Spirit of Jesus and of your love.

(Other intercessions may be offered.)
All these things we ask in the name of our Savior Jesus Christ, who taught us to pray together, saying:
Our Father... Amen.

(Or if the Lord's Prayer is not used at this point in the service)
All this we ask in the name of the Blessed and Holy Trinity. Amen.

Easter Day

Acts 10:34-43
1 Corinthians 15:19-26
John 20:1-18

Call to Worship
Leader: Give thanks to God, for God is good.
People: God's steadfast love endures forever!
Leader: God is our strength and our might.
People: God has become our salvation!
Leader: This day God has acted.
People: Let us rejoice in God's good work!

OR

Leader: Come and hear the good news!
People: What news is good today?
Leader: God has raised Jesus to new life.
People: That certainly is good news for Jesus.
Leader: It is good news for us. Hope has been raised anew.
People: We could use some good news and some hope.
Leader: Nothing is going to defeat the love and purpose of God.
People: Thanks be to God! Jesus and hope are alive forever!

Hymns and Sacred Songs
"Hope of the World"
found in:

UMH: 178	NCH: 46
H82: 472	CH: 538
PH: 360	LBW: 493

"Hymn of Promise"
found in:
UMH: 707   CH: 638
NCH: 433

"My Hope Is Built"
found in:
UMH: 368   NCH: 403
PH: 379   CH: 537
AAHH: 385   LBW: 293/294
NNBH: 274

"O God, Our Help in Ages Past"
found in:
UMH: 368   NCH: 25
H82: 680   CH: 67
AAHH: 170   LBW: 320
NNBH: 46

"O Day of Peace that Dimly Shines"
found in:
UMH: 729   PH: 450
H82: 597   CH: 711

"Sing Unto the Lord a New Song"
found in:
CCB: 16

"Your Loving Kindness Is Better than Life"
CCB: 26

Prayer for the Day / Collect
O God, who raised Jesus from death and gave the disciples hope once again, grant that we may find in his resurrection

our hope for eternal life now and forever; through Jesus Christ our Savior. Amen.

OR

We have come to rejoice and praise you, O God, for the wonder of the resurrection. We praise your name as you bring Jesus and all your people to new life and new hope. So fill us with the joy of your Spirit that we may spread the good news throughout the land. Amen.

Prayer of Confession
Leader: Let us confess to God and before one another our sins and especially our lack of faith which leads us to a life without hope.
People: We confess to you, O God, and before one another that we have sinned. We have failed to look to you for hope. We have been overwhelmed by the negative all around us. Without the hope that is grounded in you we have had nothing to share with the world. Forgive us and renew in us the good news of Easter that we may find our hope renewed and share it with all the world. Amen.
Leader: God comes to bring life, joy, and hope to all creation. God comes to claim us and renew us that we may be signs of hope for others. Rejoice in God's love and grace for you and for all creation.

Prayers of the People (and the Lord's Prayer)
We worship and adore you, O God, for the wonder of your power. You created all that is and when we rejected your life within us, you came to renew and restore us.

(The following paragraph may be used if a separate prayer of confession has not been used.)
We confess to you, O God, and before one another that we

have sinned. We have failed to look to you for hope. We have been overwhelmed by the negative all around us. Without the hope that is grounded in you we have had nothing to share with the world. Forgive us and renew in us the good news of Easter that we may find our hope renewed and share it with all the world.

We give you thanks for all the ways you express your love for us. We thank you for the beauty of the world and the joy of sharing love with one another. We thank you for hope and lives that have found new joy and fulfillment in your grace.

(Other thanksgivings may be offered.)
We pray for one another in our need and for all people anywhere who have lost hope. As you move among your children bringing new life, grant that we may be your joyful people sharing the good news of hope that is grounded in you.

(Other intercessions may be offered.)
All these things we ask in the name of our Savior Jesus Christ, who taught us to pray together, saying:
Our Father... Amen.

(Or if the Lord's Prayer is not used at this point in the service)
All this we ask in the name of the Blessed and Holy Trinity. Amen.

Easter 2

Acts 5:27-32
Revelation 1:4-8
John 20:19-31

Call to Worship
Leader: Praise God! Praise God in the sanctuary!
People: Praise God for mighty deeds!
Leader: Praise God with trumpet sound!
People: Praise God with lute and harp!
Leader: Let everything that breathes praise God!
People: Praise God for ever and ever.

OR

Leader: Come and worship God with body, mind, and Spirit.
People: I come to worship, but I have questions about God.
Leader: God welcomes you and your questions.
People: Isn't faith opposed to questions?
Leader: It actually takes faith to ask God questions.
People: Then I will come and offer myself and my questions.

Hymns and Sacred Songs
"When Our Confidence Is Shaken"
found in:
UMH: 505   CH: 534

"Faith, While Trees Are Still in Blossom"
found in:
UMH: 508   CH: 535

"Thy Word Is a Lamp"
found in:
UMH: 601	CH: 326

"Open My Eyes, that I May See"
found in:
UMH: 454	NNBH: 218
PH: 324	CH: 586

"Be Thou My Vision"
found in:
UMH: 451	NCH: 451
H82: 488	CH: 595
PH: 339

"Unity"
found in:
CCB: 59

"Open Our Eyes, Lord"
found in:
CCB: 77

Prayer for the Day / Collect
O God, who created us with reason and intellect, grant that we may use the gifts you have presented to us not to destroy faith and community but to strengthen it; through Jesus Christ our Savior. Amen.

OR

We come to worship and adore our Creator and redeemer. You have made us in your image and imparted to us a wisdom that reflects, in a small measure, your own. As we praise you and listen for your voice, so fill us with your Spirit that we may properly discern how you desire to be at work in, among, and through us. Amen.

Prayer of Confession
Leader: Let us confess to God and before one another our sins and especially our quickness to move to doubt or faith without the hard work of discernment.
People: We confess to you, O God, and before one another that we have sinned. We want things to be clear and simple. We want quick answers that comfort us and don't ask too much of us. We are glad to have someone tell us what to think as long as we already think that way. We don't want to be challenged, and we don't want to have to work out our salvation with fear and trembling. Forgive us and renew your Spirit within us that we may truly seek you and your truth. Amen.
Leader: God knows us and knows that seeking what is true and right is hard work. God grants us his Spirit so that we are able to take on the task of discernment. God invites you to drink once again from the waters of life and to be renewed in the power of the Spirit for the work ahead of you.

Prayers of the People (and the Lord's Prayer)
We worship and praise your name, O God, for the glory of your creative power. Your wisdom and knowledge are beyond our understanding and yet you have granted us the ability to share in the power of thought and reason.

(The following paragraph may be used if a separate prayer of confession has not been used.)
We confess to you, O God, and before one another that we have sinned. We want things to be clear and simple. We want quick answers that comfort us and don't ask too much of us. We are glad to have someone tell us what to think as long as we already think that way. We don't want to be challenged,

and we don't want to have to work out our salvation with fear and trembling. Forgive us and renew your Spirit within us that we may truly seek you and your truth.

We give you thanks for the glories of nature and for the way you have made us so that we can comprehend and appreciate those glories. We thank you for the ability to reason and to think and most of all for the ability to be open to your presence in creation and in our lives.

(Other thanksgivings may be offered.)
We offer into your love those who are in need of healing in mind, body, or Spirit. We pray for those who are struggling with their faith and dealing with questions about what they really believe. We pray that we may be a community of compassion, openness, and safety for those who are in the midst of their search for truth.

(Other intercessions may be offered.)
All these things we ask in the name of our Savior Jesus Christ, who taught us to pray together, saying:
Our Father... Amen.

(Or if the Lord's Prayer is not used at this point in the service)
All this we ask in the name of the Blessed and Holy Trinity. Amen.

Easter 3

Acts 9:1-6 (7-20)
Revelation 5:11-14
John 21:1-19

Call to Worship
Leader: O God, you brought up my soul from death.
People: You restored my life from those who have died.
Leader: Sing praise to God, you faithful ones.
People: We give thanks to God's holy name.
Leader: God has turned our mourning into dancing.
People: We will give thanks to God forever.

OR

Leader: Come into the presence of the Holy One.
People: It scares me to come before God.
Leader: It is right and good to fear the presence of God.
People: Should I fear because God is angry?
Leader: No. You should fear because God is love. You should fear because God wants us to grow and change.
People: It is scary to change, but I can with God's help.

Hymns and Sacred Songs
"Take My Hand, Precious Lord"
found in:
NNBH: 305

"Lord, Take My Hand and Lead Me"
found in:
LBW: 333

"Lead Me, Lord"
found in:
UMH: 473			CH: 593
AAHH: 145			Renew: 175
NNBH: 341

"Have Thine Own Way, Lord"
found in:
UMH: 382			NNBH: 206
AAHH: 449			CH: 588

"Jesus Calls Us"
found in:
UMH: 398			NCH: 171/172
H82: 549/550		CH: 337
NNBH: 183			LBW: 494

"Close to Thee"
found in:
UMH: 407			NNBH: 317
AAHH: 552/553

"Dear Lord, Lead Me Day by Day"
found in:
UMH: 411

"Change My Heart, O God"
found in:
CCB: 56			Renew: 143

"Create in Me a Clean Heart"
found in:
CCB: 54			Renew: 181/182

Prayer for the Day / Collect
O God, who desires to draw us with cords of love, grant us the grace to allow you to lead us by the hand and to be open to those you send to lead us to you; through Jesus Christ our Savior. Amen.

OR

We come to worship you, our God and our guide. We sing your praises and we look to you for the direction our lives need. We lift our hands in praise so that we can take your hand that leads us. Receive our praises and help us to walk with you in humility. Amen.

Prayer of Confession
Leader: Let us confess to God and before one another our sins and especially our unwillingness to be led by you or by anyone.
People: We confess to you, O God, and before one another that we have sinned. We are a strong-willed and stubborn people who often insist that things must be done our way. We want to be leaders, and we chafe at the idea that we may have to be followers. We even resist your efforts to lead us to a life of joy and peace. Forgive our foolishness and grant that by the power of your Spirit we may learn to quietly take your hand and follow where you lead. Amen.
Leader: God desires nothing more than our good. Whenever we are willing to let go of the reins and let God lead, God will take us where we need to go. Follow God with confidence and joy.

Prayers of the People (and the Lord's Prayer)
We glorify your name, O God, for you are the one who loves us and cares for us more deeply than we could ever

understand. You are the one who leads us to a life full of joy and peace.

(The following paragraph may be used if a separate prayer of confession has not been used.)
We confess to you, O God, and before one another that we have sinned. We are a strong-willed and stubborn people who often insist that things must be done our way. We want to be leaders, and we chafe at the idea that we may have to be followers. We even resist your efforts to lead us to a life of joy and peace. Forgive our foolishness and grant that by the power of your Spirit we may learn to quietly take your hand and follow where you lead.

We give you thanks for all the ways you have given us direction. We thank you for those who had a clearer view or who heard more precisely or who felt more deeply what you would have us to do to grow in your love, and who then faithfully shared that good news with us.

(Other thanksgivings may be offered.)
We pray for ourselves and for all, anywhere, who need to feel your loving hand leading them.

(Other intercessions may be offered.)
All these things we ask in the name of our Savior Jesus Christ, who taught us to pray together, saying:
Our Father... Amen.

(Or if the Lord's Prayer is not used at this point in the service)
All this we ask in the name of the Blessed and Holy Trinity. Amen.

Easter 4

Acts 9:36-43
Revelation 7:9-17
John 10:22-30

Call to Worship
Leader: God is our shepherd.
People: We have no other needs.
Leader: Even though I walk through the darkest valley,
People: I will fear no evil.
Leader: Surely goodness and mercy shall follow us always.
People: We shall dwell in the house of God for ever.

OR

Leader: Fear not, God is with us!
People: But the world is a scary place.
Leader: The world is scary, but God is with us.
People: The evil of the world overwhelms me.
Leader: But it doesn't overwhelm God.
People: We will trust in God and we will overcome.

Hymns and Sacred Songs
"Be Still, My Soul"
found in:
UMH: 534   NCH: 488
AAHH: 135   CH: 566
NNBH: 263

"Give to the Winds Thy Fears"
found in:
UMH: 129   PH: 286

"We Shall Overcome"
found in:
UMH: 533   NCH: 570
AAHH: 542   CH: 630
NNBH: 501

"Turn Your Eyes Upon Jesus"
found in:
UMH: 349   NNBH: 195

"Out of the Depths I Cry to You"
found in:
UMH: 515   NCH: 483
H82: 666   CH: 510
PH: 240   LBW: 295

"Hope of the World"
found in:
UMH: 178   NCH: 46
H82: 472   CH: 538
PH: 360   LBW: 493

"Leaning on the Everlasting Arms"
found in:
UMH: 133   NCH: 471
AAHH: 371   CH: 560
NNBH: 262

"O Mary, Don't You Weep"
found in:
UMH: 134

"All I Need Is You"
found in:
CCB: 100

"The Steadfast Love of the Lord"
found in:
CCB: 28   Renew: 23

Prayer for the Day / Collect
O God, who created us to live without fear in your love, grant us the grace to truly trust in your compassion and care that we may not fear anything in this life or the life to come; through Jesus Christ our Savior. Amen.

OR

We have come to this time of worship, O God, to offer our praise and thanksgiving to you. We come in awe of your greatness, and you offer to receive us in love and compassion. Help us not to fear that which is around us, since we are always held in your gracious hand. Amen.

Prayer of Confession
Leader: Let us confess to God and before one another our sins and especially the way we let our fears determine our actions.
People: We confess to you, O God, and before one another that we have sinned. We have focused our eyes on those things around us and in our fear of them, we have forsaken your path. We fear the evil things around us. We fear the thought of being poor or naked or homeless. We fear becoming ill and dying. We fear being embarrassed or ridiculed. We fear life. Forgive us and by the power of your Spirit fill us with such faith in you that we will never fear. Amen.
Leader: God's love and grace is sufficient for us. God loves us perfectly and perfect love casts out fear. May the grace of God grow in your hearts as you live bravely in the presence and power of God.

Prayers of the People (and the Lord's Prayer)
We worship you, our God and our shepherd, for you are the one who is and was and is to come. You are the eternal one who holds us safely in your own hand.

(The following paragraph may be used if a separate prayer of confession has not been used.)
We confess to you, O God, and before one another that we have sinned. We have focused our eyes on those things around us and in our fear of them, we have forsaken your path. We fear the evil things around us. We fear the thought of being poor or naked or homeless. We fear becoming ill and dying. We fear being embarrassed or ridiculed. We fear life. Forgive us and by the power of your Spirit fill us with such faith in you that we will never fear.

We give you thanks for all the times we have been aware of your presence in our midst. We give you thanks for all the times you have walked with us and carried us and we were unaware of your being there. We thank you for those you have sent to nurture and assist us in the difficult times of life. Most of all we thank you for Jesus, who came to share the good news with us that we do not need to fear, for you are always with us and for us.

(Other thanksgivings may be offered.)
We pray for those who live in fear. We know that life is hard for many who are hungry, homeless, and lost. We pray that as you encircle them with your love and care, you would enable us to be a brave presence helping them to trust you and to give up their fears.

(Other intercessions may be offered.)
All these things we ask in the name of our Savior Jesus Christ, who taught us to pray together, saying:
Our Father... Amen.

(Or if the Lord's Prayer is not used at this point in the service)
All this we ask in the name of the Blessed and Holy Trinity. Amen.

Easter 5

Acts 11:1-18
Revelation 21:1-6
John 13:31-35

Call to Worship
Leader: Praise God from the heavens!
People: Praise God from the heights!
Leader: Let all creation praise our God!
People: For God is the Creator of all!
Leader: Young and old, men and women, praise God!
People: Praise God, whose glory is above earth and heaven!

OR

Leader: Come and hear the command of our Savior.
People: Speak, Jesus; your servants are listening.
Leader: "Love one another."
People: We try to like each other.
Leader: "Love one another, as I have loved you."
People: We are your disciples; we will obey.

Hymns and Sacred Songs
"In Christ There Is No East or West"
found in:
UMH: 548
H82: 529
PH: 439/440
AAHH: 398/399
NNBH: 289
NCH: 394/395
CH: 687
LBW: 259

"Help Us Accept Each Other"
found in:

UMH: 560   NCH: 388
PH: 358   CH: 487

"Jesus, United by Thy Grace"
found in:
UMH: 561

"Father, We Thank You"
found in:
UMH: 563   H82: 302/303

"Blest Be the Dear Uniting Love"
found in:
UMH: 566

"All Creatures of Our God and King"
found in:
UMH: 62   NCH: 17
H82: 400   CH: 22
PH: 455   LBW: 527
AAHH: 147   Renew: 47
NNBH: 33

"All People that on Earth Do Dwell"
found in:
UMH: 75   NCH: 7
H82: 377/378   CH: 18
PH: 220/221   LBW: 245
NNBH: 36

"God, Whose Love Is Reigning O'er Us"
found in:
UMH: 100

"Shine, Jesus, Shine"
found in:
CCB: 81   Renew: 247

"I Am Loved"
found in:
CCB: 80

Prayer for the Day / Collect
O God, who created us to live in peace and harmony with you and with one another, grant us the grace to see you as our loving Creator and to see others as your beloved children; through Jesus Christ our Savior. Amen.

OR

We have gathered to worship you, our Creator and redeemer God, who has made us to live in communion with you and in peace with all your children. As we worship you and listen for your voice, help us not to forget that you call us to love one another as much as you call us to love you. So fill us with your loving Spirit that we will be filled with love for all creation. Amen.

Prayer of Confession
Leader: Let us confess to God and before one another our sins and especially the way we divide people into groups and judge them by whether they are like us or not.
People: We confess to you, O God, and before one another that we have sinned. You have created us for love, and yet we live most of our lives unaware of your presence. You give us every good and perfect gift, and we take and use them without giving a thought to the giver. You created us all as your children, but we act like you only love us and those just like us. Forgive us for being so fool-

ish and self-centered. Open our hearts with the power of your Spirit that we may love you more fully and love others as we love ourselves. Amen.

Leader: God does love us, each and every one. Receive the love and forgiveness of our God and remember that the same Spirit that was in Christ Jesus is now in you. Let that Spirit love the world through you.

Prayers of the People (and the Lord's Prayer)
All glory and praise is yours by right, O God, for you are the Creator of all that is and was and will be. All life comes from your life. All love comes from your love.

(The following paragraph may be used if a separate prayer of confession has not been used.)
We confess to you, O God, and before one another that we have sinned. You have created us for love, and yet we live most of our lives unaware of your presence. You give us every good and perfect gift, and we take and use them without giving a thought to the giver. You created us all as your children, but we act like you only love us and those just like us. Forgive us for being so foolish and self-centered. Open our hearts with the power of your Spirit that we may love you more fully and love others as we love ourselves.

We give you thanks for all the ways your love has touched our lives. We give you thanks that your love has made us and given us life. We thank you for the joy of creation and for the joy of living in communion with you and in community with your children. We thank you for Jesus who showed us how to love you and one another.

(Other thanksgivings may be offered.)
We pray to you for our sisters and brothers, wherever they may live. We pray that as you draw them closer to you, they

will find themselves drawn closer to others. We pray this for ourselves, as well.

(Other intercessions may be offered.)
All these things we ask in the name of our Savior Jesus Christ, who taught us to pray together, saying:
Our Father... Amen.

(Or if the Lord's Prayer is not used at this point in the service)
All this we ask in the name of the Blessed and Holy Trinity. Amen.

Easter 6

Acts 16:9-15
Revelation 21:10, 22—22:5
John 14:23-29

Call to Worship
Leader: May God be gracious to us and bless us.
People: Let the peoples praise you, O God.
Leader: Let the nations be glad and sing for joy,
People: for God judges the peoples with equity.
Leader: May God continue to bless us.
People: Let all the ends of the earth revere God.

OR

Leader: God comes among us in glory.
People: God's glory fills the earth.
Leader: God comes among us with holiness.
People: God calls us to holiness as well.
Leader: We worship the God who comes among us.
People: We join in the holy life of our God.

Hymns and Sacred Songs
"All Glory, Laud, and Honor"
found in:
UMH: 280	NNBH: 102
H82: 154/155	NCH: 216/217
PH: 88	CH: 192
AAHH: 226	LBW: 108

"Crown Him with Many Crowns"
found in:
UMH: 327   NNBH: 125

H82: 494   NCH: 301
PH: 151   CH: 234
AAHH: 288   LBW: 170

"Glorious Things of Thee Are Spoken"
found in:
UMH: 731   NCH: 307
H82: 522/523   CH: 709
PH: 446   LBW: 358
NNBH: 426

"Holy God, We Praise Thy Name"
found in:
UMH: 79   NNBH: 13
H82: 366   NCH: 276
PH: 460   LBW: 535

Prayer for the Day / Collect
O God, who is the Holy One, grant us the grace to live in holiness as you come among us in this world; through Jesus Christ our Savior. Amen.

OR

We come to worship you, the Holy One, and to welcome you into our presence. You come among us and there is no need for a temple. You are the true presence of holiness. Help us to worship you and join you in truth. Amen.

Prayer of Confession
Leader: Let us confess to God and before one another our sins and especially our inclination to worship things instead of you.
People: We confess to you, O God, and before one another that we have sinned. We have erected temples and we

have worshiped at false altars. **We have raised up wealth, fame, and greed as things to be adored. We have placed things above you and above one another. We have sacrificed each other and our own souls to gain possessions. Forgive us and call us back to worship you, the Holy One, who knows no falsehood. By the power of your Spirit let us live in truth and holiness with you. Amen.**
Leader: God knows how easily we are pulled away. God knows what we are made of. God loves us and invites us back home.

Prayers of the People (and the Lord's Prayer)
We praise and adore you, O God, for all the glory and holiness that is yours. You are the one whose actions and intentions are one.

(The following paragraph may be used if a separate prayer of confession has not been used.)
We confess to you, O God, and before one another that we have sinned. We have erected temples and we have worshiped at false altars. We have raised up wealth, fame, and greed as things to be adored. We have placed things above you and above one another. We have sacrificed each other and our own souls to gain possessions. Forgive us and call us back to worship you, the Holy One, who knows no falsehood. By the power of your Spirit let us live in truth and holiness with you.

We thank you for all the ways your steadfast love is shown to us. We thank you for being with us in good times and bad. We thank you for the times we are aware of your presence and for the times you are with us and we are oblivious.

(Other thanksgivings may be offered.)
We pray for one another in our need to center our lives in you, so that in whatever life brings us we will find wholeness

and blessing. We pray that as we open ourselves to you, we will be able to open ourselves more fully to one another.

(Other intercessions may be offered.)
All these things we ask in the name of our Savior Jesus Christ, who taught us to pray together, saying:
Our Father... Amen.

(Or if the Lord's Prayer is not used at this point in the service)
All this we ask in the name of the Blessed and Holy Trinity. Amen.

Ascension of Our Lord / Easter 7

Acts 1:1-11
Ephesians 1:15-23
Luke 24:44-53

Call to Worship
Leader: God reigns! Let the earth rejoice.
People: The heavens proclaim God's righteousness;
Leader: all the peoples behold God's glory.
People: Zion hears and is glad.
Leader: God loves those who hate evil;
People: God guards the lives of the faithful.

OR

Leader: Come and worship God with an open heart.
People: If we open our hearts, God will know who we are.
Leader: God already knows you and loves you still.
People: We come and open our hearts and lives to God.
Leader: This is the community of faith you belong to as well.
People: We will be truthful to our sisters and brothers.

Hymns and Sacred Songs
"Holy Spirit, Truth Divine"
found in:
UMH: 465   CH: 241
PH: 321   LBW: 257
NCH: 63

"I Want a Principle Within"
found in:
UMH: 410

"How Shall They Hear the Word of God"
found in:
UMH: 649

"Take My Life, and Let It Be"
found in:
UMH: 399   NCH: 448
H82: 707   CH: 609
PH: 391   LBW: 406
NNBH: 213   Renew: 150

"Only Trust Him"
found in:
UMH: 337   NNBH: 193
AAHH: 369

"O Come and Dwell in Me"
found in:
UMH: 388

"A Charge to Keep I Have"
found in:
UMH: 413   NNBH: 436
AAHH: 467/468

"O Young and Fearless Prophet"
found in:
UMH: 444   CH: 669

"Dear Jesus, in Whose Life I See"
found in:
UMH: 468

"Refiner's Fire"
found in:
CCB: 79

"Humble Yourself in the Sight of the Lord"
found in:
CCB: 72					Renew: 188

Prayer for the Day / Collect
O God, who is truth itself, grant us the grace and courage to be honest and open to you about ourselves and to not deceive others about who we are that all may know they can trust our witness through Jesus Christ our Savior. Amen.

OR

We come to worship you, O God, who dwells in truth eternal. In you there is no wavering or straying from the truth. You act out with integrity who you are, and you invite us to do the same. So fill us with your Spirit that only the truth will dwell in us, and we will be faithful witnesses of Jesus, our Savior. Amen.

Prayer of Confession
Leader: Let us confess to God and before one another our sins and especially the way we avoid the hard work of truth-telling.
People: **We confess to you, O God, and before one another that we have sinned. We have lived in deceit and falsehood. Sometimes we have boldly and knowingly lied about ourselves and about others. Sometimes we have**

"shaded" the truth, and we do it so often we usually are not even aware of it. Sometimes when we hear lies being told we do not stand up for the truth. In all these things we deny you. We place a barrier in the lives of others who learn not to trust us, and so they do not believe what we tell them about you. Forgive us and empower us with your Spirit for truth and for witness. Amen.

Leader: God delights in the truth and welcomes you into it. God loves us enough to allow us to be truthful with and about ourselves. Know that God is not deceived. God knows who we are and loves us unconditionally.

Prayers of the People (and the Lord's Prayer)
We worship and adore you, O God, for you are the very essence of truth. In you there is no shadow or turning from the truth. Because you are love, you do not need to hide yourself from us or deceive yourself about who we are. Your love is strong because there is not falsehood in your relationship with creation.

(The following paragraph may be used if a separate prayer of confession has not been used.)
We confess to you, O God, and before one another that we have sinned. We have lived in deceit and falsehood. Sometimes we have boldly and knowingly lied about ourselves and about others. Sometimes we have "shaded" the truth, and we do it so often we usually are not even aware of it. Sometimes when we hear lies being told we do not stand up for the truth. In all these things we deny you. We place a barrier in the lives of others who learn not to trust us, and so they do not believe what we tell them about you. Forgive us and empower us with your Spirit for truth and for witness.

We give you thanks for the great love with which you hold us and that enables us to live before you in honesty and truth. We thank you for those who have lived with integrity before us so that we have come to accept their testimony about you and your love.

(Other thanksgivings may be offered.)
We pray for ourselves and for others who have allowed fear to overrule love and honesty. We pray for the dispelling of that spirit of fear so that we might live with joy and honesty before your face.

(Other intercessions may be offered.)
All these things we ask in the name of our Savior Jesus Christ, who taught us to pray together, saying:
Our Father... Amen.

(Or if the Lord's Prayer is not used at this point in the service)
All this we ask in the name of the Blessed and Holy Trinity. Amen.

www.ingramcontent.com/pod-product-compliance
Lightning Source LLC
Chambersburg PA
CBHW071737040426
42446CB00012B/2382